Losing 100 pounds Naturally

Personal Insight from a Christian physician

Acknowledgements

I thank my Lord Jesus Christ in all things at all times. I thank my son and wife for their faith in me, and their support and strength. I thank my family, especially my parents, for providing me with the biblical foundation and love for God I needed to support me throughout my life.

Preface

Having struggled with obesity for years before finally reaching my ideal body weight, I have firsthand knowledge of the challenges and difficulties confronting people who are overweight. I decided to write this book because so many people, professionals and lay individuals alike, are constantly asking me what I did to lose weight. Many of these individuals have also struggled with obesity, and have tried various programs that have not been helpful. Obesity has reached epidemic proportions in the United States and is a growing problem. Obesity is a symptom of malfunction in various parts of the body and mind. For many individuals, correcting these problems is tricky. Having struggled myself for many years, I finally became successful. I have decided to share my story and personal insight in the form of a book, for those who are currently in the same position I had been for several years.

The ultimate objective of this book is to provide an easy to understand plan for overweight individuals that works well and will revitalize not only their bodies, but their spirituality, emotional well-being, and sense of purpose. This book will address weight loss from my unique perspective as a specialist physician (Child Neurologist) who understands the role of the mind and brain in the battle over illness. As a health-conscious Christian, I also incorporate a biblical perspective for wellness and weight loss. I explain obesity through the RESTORATION model. It has helped me, and can also be valuable to you.

Table of Contents

Chapter 1-Introduction   11
Chapter 2-My Slim Years   15
Chapter 3-Becoming Fat   29
Chapter 4-Why I needed to lose weight ASAP   35
Chapter 5-What I did to lose 100 lbs   39
Chapter 6-Reversing obesity using the RESTORATION
         Model   49
Chapter 7-Practical Application of the RESTORATION
         Model: Prescription for Health and Healing 67
Chapter 8-Conclusion   101

Chapter 1: Introduction

I was more than 100 pounds overweight, and believe me, I was unhappy. As a physician who spends a great deal of time convincing patients of the importance of health and nutrition, I was not a good role model. I had various problems associated with obesity including sleep apnea, back pain, insomnia, fatigue, and heartburn/gastroesophageal reflux. I had to make sure some antacid was available at night or else... I was frequently out of breath after mildly strenuous activities. The worse part was the psychological implication of my obesity. My self-image was poor, despite a convincing façade of self confidence. I took any joke or comment about obesity personally.

I knew I had to do something about my weight, but I did not know what? How? Where should I start? Needless to say, I was one step away from depression. I was certainly dissatisfied, embarrassed and confused. I had been very obese for many years, and felt trapped and hopeless. I felt that the huge stress in my life as a very busy Pediatric Neurologist played a great role in my obesity. But was that just an excuse?

Now fast forward a few years. Now, I have lost 100 pounds and look and feel GREAT! Many of my patients do not even recognize me. I have tremendous energy, no heartburn, no backache, no fatigue, and no sleep apnea. In fact, I have no sleep problems at all. My self-image is good, and I have been totally transformed physically, mentally and spiritually.

Introduction

The problem of obesity is very intricate. There are multiple abnormal variables present in individuals with chronic obesity. We know that genes play a definite role. I have often compared myself to my wife. She eats often, but she never seems to put on any weight, regardless of her activity level or the foods she eats (in reality she is very health conscious). In my case, it seems that just looking at food could make me gain weight. Although my wife eats all of the time, she eats in small portions. She has a good appetite, but can only eat a small amount at a time. She has what I call a **"small sac"** (or stomach), despite having a healthy appetite. In my case, not only do I have a **"big sac"**, that is the room to eat large amounts, but I also have a big appetite. That is a dangerous combination.

The problem of weight gain is of course more complex than the capacity of your *sac* or the size of your appetite. Our genetic make up determines more than our physical or structural constitution, it plays a role in the efficiency of our metabolism.

Apart from innate factors, environmental (that is external) variables are very important. I will show how environmental factors play a huge role when it comes to weight issues. Stress, psychosocial conditioning, nutrition, lifestyle and the presence of metabolic/endocrine disturbances are all important. Despite the complexity of obesity, it can be overcome as it was in my case.

Chapter 2: My Slim Years

I was most fit when I lived in Africa, particularly in Rwanda. My family and I moved to Africa when I was 11 years old to do missionary work. Prior to going to Africa I was not obese, but I was somewhat heavily built. After a few months of living in Rwanda, I found that I became thin and muscular without exerting any effort. Looking back, my lifestyle was such that it would have been almost impossible for me to become overweight. Regarding exercise, I did not need to workout since many physical activities were automatically built into my daily routine. Our only mode of transportation was our two legs. We did not own a car. Someone did lend us a motorcycle for a while, but we used it for recreational purposes only. We walked everywhere including to the marketplace, which was approximately five miles away. We went to the marketplace once a week. In school, we did a lot of agricultural work. This was built into our curriculum. No one owned a television. We only had electricity between 6-9 pm each day. We could not be idle even if we tried.

Our eating pattern was interesting. I remember eating a lot but I simply would not gain weight. At one point, I remember being teased by a classmate for being so thin. I ate a lot of fruits and vegetables. We had a large garden and grew a variety of vegetables. Everything was "organic", and the majority of our foods were unprocessed. Most of what we drank was water. To a much lesser extent, we drank pure fruit juice (usually freshly made from fruits in our garden). Prior to going to Africa, we enjoyed sodas and drinks but that was simply not as conveniently available where we were in Rwanda. We did drink sodas occasionally for very special occasions.

We got plenty of rest each night because we automatically went to bed around 9 pm when our electricity was cut off. We did have the option to stay up later using a lantern, but there was no reason to. There was not much else to do after the lights went off and we were usually tired by the day's physical activities. In Rwanda we had very little stress. That concept was foreign to us. My family and I were never in a rush in the small village-like setting where we lived. It was as laid back as you could ever imagine. It was very different from living in New York City where I was born and had lived most of my life prior to that point.

The foods we ate were very nourishing. I ate all I wanted. I ate until I was full. The fruits and vegetables were free of pesticides, and were of high quality. The fruits were vine-ripened and tasted very good. We ate a large variety of legumes, peas, beans and fruits, some of which I had never heard of before. It was in Africa, especially Rwanda, where I learned to like fruits such as mango and avocado.

I remember that when we had first arrived in Rwanda, the more established missionaries had a tradition of inviting new comers to their house on a rotational basis for a few days. We were invited one day by a neighbor to dine at their home. A delicious sandwich was prepared; I had never tasted a sandwich such as that. I remember asking before I ate the sandwich what was in it. But I was told to taste it first. It was a green spread. I planned to take a bite and then politely say that I did not want anymore. When I started eating the sandwich, however, it had a great taste with spices that were unusual. After I ate a couple sandwiches, I was finally told that it was avocado (guacamole). From that time on I looked at avocadoes in a new light. I also did not like onions prior to going to Africa. When we moved to Africa, someone prepared a dish with cassava and raw onions that was quite good. From that time on, I developed a new taste for onions.

Back in the States, I had enjoyed all types of potato chips (preferably barbecue or something spicy). I could tolerate onions only if they were onion rings. Cookies, candy, ice cream were things

I could live on back then. My parents were very health conscious when I was young, but I was not. In Africa, we had no choice but to eat healthy, unprocessed and a lot of raw foods. We had no choice but to drink plenty of water. That is mostly what we had. Since we were very active and worked outdoors a lot, we were often thirsty. So drinking plenty of water daily was automatic. With the above lifestyle, it was impossible to be overweight. I was the thinnest I had ever been in my life.

I share this part of my life because I realize that lifestyle is very important when it comes to weight management. In my case, I was fortunate back then that I was in an environment where I had no choice but to be fit. Since in Africa we did not have many options, I did not get tempted to consume certain foods or drinks.

Since we did not have a car, we had to walk. Our legs were our natural locomotion all the time. By the end of the day we did not have any sleep problems, because we were tired from our physical labors. All of our calories were expended. We did not have to worry about heartburn or indigestion.

Interestingly, when my family moved to Ivory Coast (in the west coast of Africa) we felt like we were moving from farm land to city dwelling. We lived in the second largest city in that country. It was more modernized. We had electricity 24 hours a day 7 days a week. We had a car. We had access to television, although we did not personally own one. There were more processed foods. I still remained very fit without any effort being expended. Retrospectively, we still ate plenty of fresh raw fruits and vegetables. We were always physically active. We chose to walk to school, even though it was several miles away. And water was still our primary beverage, although we had greater access to sodas and juices.

While in Ivory Coast, however, we went on furlough (vacation) for the first time. We returned to the United States for 3 months. I was 13 years old at that time. The first thing our well-meaning concerned relatives asked was 'what happen to you, why are you so thin, did you not have any food to eat while you were in Africa?' Then they started fattening us up with food, lots of it. The foods we ate were not raw or fresh. Instead, they were overly processed. We indulged in television and became 'couch potatoes'. This was our way of having a good vacation, or as our relatives said 'recovering' from our stay in Africa.

Needless to say, when we got back to Ivory Coast, after our vacation, my twin brother and I were almost unrecognizable. The reaction of our African friends was one of laughter. "What happened to you guys?" We had gained so much weight that it was funny and sad at the same time. After only a few weeks of resuming our normal activities in Ivory Coast; we burned off all the excess fat and calories. We did not consciously try to workout or diet. We simply got back to our previous routine and the weight came off very quickly. We were able to wear our old clothes again.

What happened to me in Africa is quite interesting because it highlights several important factors pertaining to weight balance and obesity:

1) **Metabolism is highly influenced by lifestyle.** As an adolescent, my metabolism was probably fast anyway. But in Africa, I did things that allowed it to work optimally, proper nutrition with fresh, raw, live fruits and vegetables, and unprocessed foods. Hydration with plenty of water, daily exercise/physical activity and adequate rest. When I came back to the States on vacation, my lifestyle changed dramatically. I put on a lot of weight *automatically*. When I went back to Africa, I again changed my metabolism, effortlessly by returning to the lifestyle that I had previously adopted, and the weight came off effortlessly.

2) **Changes happen for the best or the worst.** The fact that I had a wonderful lifestyle in Africa and that I was fit, did not prevent me from gaining a lot of weight when I came back to the States. My life style changed in the States. I was protected from obesity only as long as my lifestyle supported proper fat metabolism. Although I gained a lot of weight on my furlough, I was able to lose it when I returned to my previous lifestyle. Although genes play a role, I believe that the majority of overweight individuals are largely affected by their lifestyle when it comes to obesity and weight gain.

3) **Lifestyle is like a machine where all the parts are essential for proper functioning.** When one is concerned about weight loss, you can not just focus on nutrition, you cannot just focus on exercise, you cannot just focus on dietary supplements, and you cannot just focus on moderation in eating. *All* of these components are important. They all must be focused on at the same time and incorporated altogether.

4) **Weight management should be incorporated in one's natural lifestyle.** Although there are certain things that can be done to speed up ones metabolism in order to burn fat quickly, the goal should be to adopt a *lifestyle* that can be maintained permanently and is healthy.

5) **Wellness is <u>absolute</u> instead of relative.** You are either well or you are not. The door is either closed or it is opened. Proper lifestyle is a whole package where all of the ingredients are important. Moreover, each element supports the other in a synergistic fashion.

When I lived in Africa, I had very little stress, especially compared to what I would experience in the next few years in the States. Stress-free living is a vital part of health, wellness and weight management. In addition to physical and mental health, my spiritual health was great. Spiritual health is important for mental health, which in turn supports physical well-being.

Chapter 3- Becoming Fat

My journey to obesity began around the same time I started experiencing stress, developed a sedentary lifestyle, and began eating processed foods. When I came back from Africa, after living there for 7 years, I enrolled as a premedical student in Michigan. Up until I started medical school, my weight was fairly good. I did start gaining weight almost as soon as I returned from Africa, but it was a slow, gradual process. During medical school, however, there was an exponential increase in my weight that persisted throughout medical school and residency, worsened during my medical specialty training, and finally got out of hand in my first few years of starting medical practice.

In my case, everything that could go wrong went wrong. I ate the wrong foods and lots of it. Because my schedule was a very busy one, I often started my day very early, sometimes at 5 am. After eating a late meal at night, I had no desire to eat breakfast. It was too early to eat any way, I felt. I convinced myself that by skipping breakfast I could lose a few calories. Of course, I knew better than that. But skipping breakfast was one of many harmful things that I did back then. I knew, as a physician, that breakfast was the most important meal of the day. But I was not 'set up' to eat breakfast under the circumstances I was in. I became progressively more sedentary. The only exercise I got was walking from patient room to patient room or along the hospital hallways. Occasionally, I bought exercise equipment.

Unfortunately, I did not use them consistently. One excuse was that I just did not have enough time. Getting started was also hard since I was so out of shape.

My stress level increased, as only the stress level of a busy physician can. Television did not help at all. Since I was often overworked, when I did have time to relax, I often chose the mindless activity of watching television. To really feel relaxed, I felt that I needed to eat something 'yummie' while watching television. Not surprisingly, I could eat and eat and eat while watching television. I felt that I had to eat throughout the entire time I watched television. I often fell asleep at night while watching television. Chronic stress is a harmful thing. I view it as a destructive and disruptive energy that forces you to have maladaptive behaviors, overeating being one of them. Chronic stress is, unfortunately, built-in the process of going through medical school, residency and specialty training.

During most of my specialty training in Child Neurology I worked excessively. On many occasions I held 2 phones to my head responding to 2 urgent calls simultaneously. I worked long hours. I did enjoy my training experience very much. So much that I seldom minded the difficulty of what I had to go through. But there was a price to pay. Overeating became an unhealthy way, it seemed, to relieve stress.

I had another problem. Although I had an insatiable appetite, that appetite was surpassed only by my visual attraction to good food. Meaning, that if there was something that looked good or that I liked, I felt that I had to have it right then and there. I also did not like to waste. Having lived in Africa, I became conscious of our exaggerated tendency to waste food in the States. When it came to food, this meant eating everything. As mentioned above, there was a time I could eat all I wanted and not gain weight. Now was not that time. Many of the foods I found myself eating were packed with empty calories. Looking back, I remember relatives that would insist I ate all my food, even when I was not hungry. I often wondered if that did not have an adverse effect on me. I felt that I had to clean my plate even if I was full. Often, there are psychological influences that affect our eating habits.

Everything in my life seemed to conspire to transform me from a built and fit man, to being corpulent and unhealthy. I might have escaped the problem of obesity if I ate the right foods, or perhaps if I remained physically active. I might even have been protected against obesity if I did not have to deal with chronic stress. With all of the above problems mounting each year, however, I had no chance. I was doomed. I also did not have 'slim' genes to rely on.

Chapter 4: Why I Needed to Loose Weight ASAP

I cannot think of one advantage to being fat. But I know countless reasons why being obese is problematic. In my case, although I appeared healthy on the surface, I had a variety of health illnesses. I did not sleep well because of snoring (which also affected my wife's quality of sleep), insomnia and reflux. I ate late at night and relied on antacids many nights to get me through until the next morning. Because I received poor quality sleep, this meant that I had excessive daytime sleepiness or hypersomnolence constantly. Driving long distances was hazardous. I was often out of breath, even for some activities that were not strenuous.

My well-meaning wife who is also a physician kept giving me advice regarding what I should do to lose weight. I knew everything that she was saying was true, but I felt powerless to comply. My twin brother who is also a physician reminded me that I could become diabetic if I did not lose weight. Of course, as a physician I knew these things. But as an internist who deals with diabetics everyday, my brother was particularly concerned about his brother's welfare. I had significant truncal obesity that put me at serious risk for diabetes, heart disease, gastritis and back pain. Thinking about the health ramifications of my obesity brought me great trepidation. In addition to diabetes, I thought of cardiac problems, endocrine abnormalities such as thyroid dysfunction, impaired immune function and various other health problems that could only lead to one eventuality, a premature death.

As a person dealing with obesity, the worse part was the psychological component. My self-perception, self-esteem and self-worth suffered immensely. Not only was I a physician, but I was one who always spoke to my patients about wellness and proper life style. What type of example was I setting for my patients? I had a hard time counseling my obese patients to lose weight when I needed to lose weight as much or more than they did. Being obese gave me a great feeling of inadequacy that was almost unbearable.

I also had a spiritual concern. By being as overweight as I was, that meant that I was intemperate and lacked self-control. A glutton, and on the wrong path. How could I serve God effectively when His temple, my body, was overwhelmed with blubber? Was I violating the commandment that says: "thou shalt have no other gods before me"? Perhaps food had become an edible god for me. Although I knew that God still loved me, I felt that I was not presenting myself to God in an acceptable way. I knew that I could not serve Him as well as I could if I were fit in body, mind and spirit. I felt it was time to put God to the test.

Chapter 5: What I Did to Lose 100 lbs

Preparation phase

Preparation is very important in any weight loss program. One has to really *want* to lose weight, and be prepared to do whatever it takes to do so. In addition, one has to really be ready mentally. It is very important not to set oneself up for failure. One has to set goals, plan well, and engage in a routine that is practical not only in the short run but also long-term. In my case, I wanted to choose a program that I knew would work. I did not want to do something that would be too difficult, expensive or time-consuming.

The first thing I did was to imagine what life would be like if I were thin and at my ideal body weight. For a few seconds I experienced immense joy at the thought of how life would be if I were fit. I decided to fast. For four days, I ate nothing. I only drank water. The main purpose of the fast was to ask God for strength. I needed commitment and stamina. I needed to be perseverant. I absolutely did not want to fail in this endeavor and did not trust my own strength to become successful. During my fast, I prayed frequently, asking God for help. If God would hear my cry, the battle would be won.

Interestingly, after a day or two of fasting, I was so hungry that I longed for the time where I would be able to eat anything. That meant that I could have a fresh start at eating healthy foods. It was as if my taste buds had a chance to reset themselves.

Induction phase

After the fast, much prayer and meditation, I was finally ready to start. My plan was to eat the right types of foods, the right amount and at the right time. I decided to drink plenty of water. I designed an exercise program that was fun and that I could do long-term. At first I tried the treadmill. I was faithful with it for several weeks, but decided that I would be more comfortable walking each morning for one hour. The problem I had was that I felt I needed to walk for at least one hour to get the right amount of exercise needed. This was based on the fact that I did not want to walk very fast and was going to use the walk as my time for prayer and meditation. It seemed, at first, that walking a whole hour was not a realistic goal since I wanted to do it early in the morning and since my day usually starts very early. I started walking 15 minutes a day, then 20 minutes, then 30 minutes. Eventually I ended up walking 2 hours each day, waking up at 3 o'clock in the morning to reach that goal. Walking 2 hours in the morning and starting at 3am was fueled by the spiritual aspect of my walk.

Walking very early in the morning allowed me to pray and meditate in a way that was nothing less than transformative. I was able to appreciate the beauty of the starry sky with the intermittent entertainment of shooting stars. It became inevitable for me to study nature while walking. This helped me mentally. Walking is, a good way to relieve stress, ponder on the previous day's experiences, and plan ahead for the next day. The experience of walking allowed me to drink more water, which helped my bowels to function better. I started sleeping better. In short, walking became an indispensable part of my day. By walking I got my exercise, prayer, meditation, relaxation and many other benefits such as the study of nature. I found that, somehow, I was able to work more efficiently. I was able to come home earlier. I also went for late afternoon walks and weekend walks with my family. That improved our family quality time. Weekend and afternoon walks also allowed me to get some good sunlight. Sunlight is important for mood, boosting the immune system and vitamin D production.

I had to make some important and strategic changes when it came to eating though. I decided to never skip breakfast, since breakfast is the most important meal of the day. To accomplish this,

I had to eat lightly at night, and as early as possible. This meant that since I spend a good portion of the night with a relatively empty stomach, I would be hungry by morning. During which time I would be able to *break the fast* of the previous evening or eat breakfast. I decided to drink plenty of water that is at least 80 ounces of water, often more, daily. I bought water bottles to my office daily that I filled with water and drank constantly between patients.

I started taking dietary supplements using a system called *Glycolean* that provided glyconutrients, minerals, vitamins, antioxidants and various other nutrients that support fat burning and are all natural. This system also allowed me to find out about low glycemic foods, that is foods that do not illicit a large insulin release which would otherwise result in fat storage. I viewed taking the supplements as an adjunct or a part of an overall wellness and weight loss program.

After doing the above for several days, I had mixed emotions. It seemed like I had a very long road ahead, considering that I wanted to go from obese to lean. A few weeks after starting my program, I was starting to lose weight; one patient said to me, I see you are gaining weight. Comments like these, at the early phase of my weight loss journey, were somewhat distracting. But I knew I had to go forward. While it felt like I had a marathon ahead of me, on the one hand, I felt that the victory was already won on the other. I was engaged in a routine that I could follow with little stress and that would, in the future, cause a radical transformation. I was thrilled!

Maintenance phase

Losing weight is one thing. Keeping it off is another. A few years ago when I was in residency training, I had decided to go on a raw diet for one month. I only ate raw fruits and vegetables and drank only water. I exercised daily. At the end of the month, I lost approximately 40 pounds, only to gain it back with interest, shortly thereafter. I did not want the same situation to occur again. I wanted to lose weight and keep it off. What I found is that by continuing with my program, my metabolism had become fast and efficient. I still have temptations, but the battle is won!

The biggest challenges come when my daily routine is broken. For instance, when I travel. Since I do not want to regress and gain the weight back, in my daily walk I always ask God for strength daily.

Chapter 6: Reversing Obesity Using the RESTORATION Model

Are you having problems losing weight? Does it seem like you are fighting a hopeless cause? Let me share with you a model that will help with more than weight loss. It will show you how you can be transformed or restored totally to wellness!

My wife and I have developed a RESTORATION model of health and healing that is dynamic comprehensive and integrative. The model as it pertains to obesity, which I consider an illness and various other health challenges, is explained as follows:

❖ The RESTORATION model is based on a deep understanding of biopsychosociospiritual factors.

- Instead of focusing on just biological causes of illness and dysfunction, it also looks at psychological, social and spiritual causes. It works both ways: biological disturbances can affect our mental well-being and disrupt our social milieu. This in turn can adversely affect our spirituality. The reverse is also true.

- A primarily spiritual problem can trickle down and affect every aspect of our existence including ones that appear biologically-based. A person who is failing to lose weight by focusing primarily on biomedical factors may be more successful if pychosociospiritual factors are considered. Although a greater acceptance and appreciation of psychosocial factors has occurred in the past few years, spiritual concerns are poorly understood and often ignored.

o Spirituality is crucial when it comes to all health problems, a perfect example being that of obesity. Spiritual virtues such as faith, humility, love, peace and joy can be thought of as **spiritual vitamins** that may be deficient and causing problems.

o Negative attitudes and emotions such as chronic fear and

guilt, resentment, a desire for revenge, and pessimism are examples of **spiritual toxins** that provide the need for spiritual detoxification and cleansing.

o Negative emotions may do any or all of the following:

- Interfere with sleep
- Cause gastrointestinal symptoms
- Cause hypertension (high blood pressure)
- Cause headaches
- Cause anxiety symptoms
- Cause mood disorder
- Cause chronic diseases
- Cause fatigue

- Impair memory and concentration

Negative emotions can also lead to such devastating illnesses as strokes and heart attacks if there are certain additional risk factors present. Apart from the physical complications of obesity, there are primary emotional problems that can have dire consequences also. Secondary emotional factors develop which complicates the overall presentation of obesity.

Instead of living with chronic fear and guilt, or other negative feelings, if someone decides to place their faith in God with the belief that He is all powerful, that person can experience healing. For example, that person's blood pressure may decrease. They may gain peace, happiness, joy, and become empowered to reach their goal of losing weight.

Faith is also vital. It is interesting to note that Christ, when He was on earth, accomplished numerous miracles. He often would say "your faith has made you whole". Faith **must** be important for Jesus to have made this statement repeatedly. Faith is more than belief. It is an active, dynamic process that allows an individual to have access to healing that would otherwise not be possible. In my situation, I believe that through prayer, fasting and faith, Christ was able to make me whole by renewing my mind, granting me the will and time to exercise daily and consistently providing the insight and strength needed to totally alter my lifestyle. In the process, Jesus gave me instant peace, trust and the realization that weight loss was now just a matter of time and was inevitable.

- ❖ The RESTORATION model is holistic.

    o Full restoration is only possible if all factors that may be contributing to illness are taken into consideration. This includes biological, psychological, social and spiritual. In addition, total restoration, as far as biology is concerned, requires an approach that works *with*, instead of against, the body. Covering up or suppressing a symptom with drugs is not the same as correcting a nutritional deficiency or avoiding food toxins that may be causing the problem in the first place.

o Imagine a person with chronic hypertension, lupus, diabetes or migraine headaches being told: 'Your condition is chronic, and life-long. We do not know why you have that problem. You will need to take these pills for the rest of your life. You had better be compliant with this drug'. As opposed to a person who is told 'There are various problems that may be contributing to your condition including dietary, life style, stress and genetic predisposition.
While we may not be able to alter your genes, there are many ways that we can help

encourage your body's natural healing mechanisms or *the doctor within* by the grace of God. God is able to help you, and I will do what I can to assist you'. Everything the body needs for proper functioning such as proper nutrition, proper hydration with water, exercise, good social and spiritual support, adequate rest, and temperance is vital not only for maintenance of optimal wellness but also for the re-establishment of total health.

- ❖ The RESTORATION model is etiologic-based

  - o Complete return to health cannot occur unless the underlying problem is addressed.

The body has an innate healing mechanism that usually allows it to carry out its own curative action, independent of medical intervention. A good example is a viral upper respiratory or ear infection for which an antibiotic (useless against viral infections) is prescribed for two weeks. After two weeks the individual gets better because the viral infection is terminated and overcome by the immune system. Coincidentally, the antibiotic was prescribed for the same length of time. A misinformed patient might, thus, sing the praises of a drug that did not do anything to cure them. People must realize that illness is not a medication deficiency problem. A headache is not caused by ibuprofen deficiency any more than heartburn is caused by a ranitidine (Zantac) deficiency.

- Headaches can be caused by numerous factors, often related to nutrition and life style that could easily be corrected without medication. With obesity, there are a variety of factors that are involved. Each issue must be addressed in order for obesity to be permanently overcome.

- What about genes? Genes are indeed very

important in the manifestation of most illnesses, obesity included. But genetics is just one factor. At best, genes may cause a greater susceptibility or vulnerability in an individual, but with proper life style, attitude, nutrition and some spiritual help, the genetic vulnerability may remain just that, *vulnerability*. Yes, when it comes to weight some people have to struggle more than others. Unlike my wife, who can eat whatever she wants, whenever she wants, and remain thin. It would seem that just looking at food makes me gain weight. Despite the fact that there are obese individuals on both sides of my family, I was able, by using the principles of the RESTORATION model, to lose 100 lbs.

o There is, in fact, no *sickness gene*. There are no genes that exist to cause disease. Instead, when some genes are abnormally expressed or mutated, they can code for proteins that cause metabolic derangements that result in illness. Because genetic disturbances make it more difficult for some individuals to be healthy that is one among many reasons that we should never judge others based on their weight, health status or other difficulties they may be experiencing.

- o In reality, if you look at all of the individuals that are taken to the doctor's office or the hospital and examine the actual cause of their disease, the etiology is often nutrition, life style or stress related. Statistically then, addressing *these* issues thoroughly should result in restoration of health.

❖ The RESTORATION model is curative.

- o Instead of being palliative, our model is restorative. It is based on the understanding that total healing is possible, even though in some cases it would seem to require a miracle. In difficult cases Divine intervention may be the only avenue to obtain a cure. This model places no limitations on the possibility of healing, even for the most refractory cases. Healing is not predicated on diagnosis, chronicity, cause, genetic vulnerability, or virulence. Instead, the level of faith, prayer, and God's willingness to intervene are the most important factors. This model is one that should bring hope and comfort.

o Although a cure is never out of reach, a

cure may not always be God's will. In a broad spiritual context, sometimes some good may come out of a person's afflictions. Good for the person, or others around them. The illness may be temporary. Someone who is going through a chronic illness and understands the RESTORATION model would be equipped to face the illness with a positive attitude and hope. Hope, by itself, may contribute to healing.

- You must always be willing to take responsibility for your actions. In many cases, violating a simple health principle may lead to illness, with

> secondary, tertiary and quaternary problems compromising health further. A miracle or Divine intervention should never be expected, if there is willful and persistent violation of health laws.

The RESTORATION model is very complete. In order for its application to have positive effects, it must be understood in its entirety. All of the principles in the model are important. The model cannot be fully effective if a few principles are applied and others are ignored. These principles work together. They are all interrelated. Applying all of the principles will cause synergistic results.

Chapter 7: Practical Application of the RESTORATION model: Prescription for Health and Healing

RESTORATION is also used as an acronym that describes very specifically the steps and factors needed to obtain a full return to health:

R – RENEWAL

"Create in me a pure heart, O God, and renew a steadfast spirit within me."
Ps 51:10

When it comes to chronic obesity, no real improvement can occur without the renewal of the mind; this is where it all starts. There needs to be a renewal of attitude and approach toward wellness. Acquiring an understanding that obesity, mild, moderate or severe is a conquerable problem may *already* initiate some very positive changes toward weight loss.

A renewal entails a complete change, a makeover, a total alteration. This is a type of change that can only come from God. Even with individuals who possess an inner strength to change, that willpower and inner strength are a gift from God. Many individuals with chronic obesity, unfortunately, feel, helpless and hopeless. Such individuals are in desperate need of total renewal of mind and body. If you have a problem with obesity, start with the recognition that there is a problem which must be corrected. Whether you have mild obesity or whether you are several hundred pounds overweight, the following applies:

- ❖ Ask God for help. Ask God to bring a total renewal of your mind and body. God is the author

Practical Application of the RESTORATION model:
Prescription for Health and Healing

of all good things and is very willing to help you.
- You must be willing to surrender to God entirely. Follow God's laws, religious as well as those that are health-related.
- Start exercising faith. God is in control, always. He can give you the mastery that you need.
- A renewal requires being humble. If you are proud, your pride may interfere with divine intervention.
- Total renewal requires having a forgiving heart. Lack of forgiveness of self or others can disrupt proper mental health. Good mental health is a requirement for successful weight loss.
- A total renewal entails a full commitment for a lifestyle change. You must believe that change

is possible with the help of God.
- ❖ Avoid procrastination. Do not start tomorrow. Get started right now!
- ❖ It is important to remain focused, and not get distracted by negative thoughts or predictions. Instead of focusing on your current shortcomings, contemplate you future success.

E – EXERCISE

"Six days you shall labor and do all your work"
Exodus 20: 9

Exercise is vital. You must make time to exercise. There should be absolutely no excuse when it comes to exercise. Whether you have a very hectic schedule or are bed-ridden, you should still exercise. You may need to start slowly. Discuss an exercise program with your

Practical Application of the RESTORATION model:
Prescription for Health and Healing

physician if you are unfit or have heart disease, but exercise.

By exercising, you turn on a powerful system that does the following:

- ✓ Burns fat calories
- ✓ Speeds your metabolism
- ✓ Restores your energy
- ✓ Improves your quality of sleep
- ✓ Helps your bowels to work better
- ✓ Helps with detoxification of your body by eliminating harmful toxins using virtually every organ in the body.
- ✓ Enhances your immune and endocrine (hormone) systems.

In addition to the above, you are also boosting many mental and spiritual functions as well. Exercise is a good way to fight stress and improve mood. Because consistency is essential, I recommend a very simple exercise that can be continued throughout your life with multiple benefits and that has worked for me:

- **Walk** for 1 hour early every morning at approximately the same time each day.
- Walk at a pace that is convenient and comfortable for you.
- If possible, choose a place or trail that is not noisy and where you can be exposed to nature.
- Take the opportunity to breathe deeply and walk upright.
- Use that time to pray and meditate. This is an ideal time to talk to the Creator.
- Try to appreciate nature during your walk (e.g. the stars in the sky, other celestial bodies, the vegetation, etc.).
- Drink plenty of water after each walk.

Practical Application of the RESTORATION model: Prescription for Health and Healing

❖ Apart from your daily walk, consider taking the stairs instead of the elevator. Do not get upset if you can not park very close to the grocery store. Walking a little distance can only help. Use every opportunity to remain active.

S – SELF-CONTROL

"Do you not know that your body is a temple of the Holy Spirit, who is in you, whom you have received from God? You are not your own; you were bought at a price. Therefore honor God with your body." I Co 6: 19, 20

Self-control, or temperance, is of vital importance. Self-control can apply to many areas of your life including time, ingestion of toxic substances (e.g.

tobacco, recreational alcohol), speech (inability to hold ones tongue), and the indulgence of appetite. If you lack self-control with regard to appetite, it can lead to the following troublesome circumstances: you start to overeat, usually the wrong kind of foods→ your quality of sleep deteriorates due to obstructive sleep apnea and heart burn→ You become chronically tired with concentration and memory problems→ it becomes difficult to exercise since you are always exhausted → you gain more weight due to lack of exercise and become grouchy and depressed and want to eat even more. Self-esteem and self-image start to suffer. Everything spirals downward... Unfortunately this is a common scenario. For help with self-control, I recommend the following:

Practical Application of the RESTORATION model: Prescription for Health and Healing

- ❖ Recognize that your body is not your own but God's. Realize that when God's spirit fully dwells in the temple (which is your body, your mind, and your brain) it is very difficult to remain overweight, to have stress or to have spiritual dysfunctions. In other words, full restoration can be expected.
- ❖ Be aware that if *self* is not in control, something else automatically is. Always try to identify what that *something* is that is controlling you.
- ❖ As always, you should not hesitate to ask God for help.
- ❖ Eat nutritious foods. These can be restorative but also delicious. With a little effort and planning, you can find foods that are healthy, support weight loss and are tasty. By following

all of God's health laws, the brain and mind are able to function well. In many cases, just by following natural health laws, the problem of self-control can be conquered.
- ❖ Obtaining self-control may take time and effort but God can certainly provide assistance and lessen your struggle.
- ❖ Giving up should never be an option! If you make a mistake, start again and keep trying.

T – TIME

"There is a time for everything and a season for every activity under heaven." Ecclesiastes 3:1

Time is one of the greatest gifts we have. Time can be very profitable and beneficial if used wisely. When it comes to restoration, time is always an important factor. When you commit to fitness and take all of the appropriate steps toward reaching that goal, at that moment the battle is more than halfway won. Getting on the right path is more important than reaching ones destination because given time you will get there by the grace of God.

God's timetable is different than ours. He may choose to take longer than you would prefer, or He may take care of your problem much sooner than you could ever imagine. In each case, God is the master coordinator and knows what He is doing. All you need to do is exercise patience and trust. With respect to time, I recommend the following:

❖ Make the right lifestyle changes now! Do not procrastinate since it will only get harder to

change with the passage of time.
- ❖ Be patient, always.
- ❖ Although God's timing is different than ours, His timetable is undeniably better.
- ❖ It is more important to commit to change than to focus on the time it takes to reach your goal. You will eventually get there!
- ❖ God does not operate in the confines of human time. Place your entire trust in Him.
- ❖ Healing takes only as long as it takes for **God's** agenda to be completed.

O – OBEDIENCE

"As obedient children, do not conform to the evil desires you had when you lived in ignorance." 1Peter 1:14

Obedience is crucial when it comes to restoration.

Practical Application of the RESTORATION model:
Prescription for Health and Healing

Unfortunately, disease does not discriminate between willful disobedience and one that stems from ignorance. The end result of disobedience to natural health laws is the same. Because illness is a personal matter, it is imperative that each individual take responsibility for learning everything necessary regarding their health. Obedience may prevent illness completely.

The first place to start is with obedience to God's laws. God's all inclusive laws are designed to provide optimal health in all areas, spiritual, physical and mental. Adam and Eve were given instructions on the type of foods to eat that would allow proper function not only of their body but also of their mind. This would allow them to properly commune with their Creator, the most important aspect of wellness. As with disobedience pertaining to other rules, there are consequences, sometimes severe ones when it comes to health. The consequences may be immediate, or they may be delayed and insidious in their onset. It is never too late to start obeying God's laws. It is also important to realize that:

- ❖ Obedience, in general, is a safeguard against self-destruction and harm.
- ❖ Health laws come in one package that must be kept entirely.
- ❖ Obedience involves trust and confidence that the health laws given are beneficial. Natural laws are restorative. However, never confuse nature with the God of nature. Only God is infallible and omnipotent.
- ❖ Obedience to proper health laws is voluntary

Practical Application of the RESTORATION model:
Prescription for Health and Healing

but only temporarily so. You can choose to obey now or be forced to obey later.

❖ Obedience to health laws is synonymous with health promotion, health maintenance and disease prevention. None of these are passive acts. Effort is required.

❖ Obedience to health laws may be viewed as an investment for future wellness.

❖ By full obedience to God's law, you can go from being morbidly obese to reaching your ideal body weight, naturally.

R – REST

> "There remains, then, a Sabbath-rest for the people of God"
> Hebrews 4:9

Rest in all forms is important. Without adequate rest, full restoration is impossible. When resting or relaxing, one can recuperate physically, mentally, and spiritually. There are in fact several types of rests:

1- Sleep. Sleep is very important because it allows reparation from the wear and tear encountered throughout the day. During deep sleep, important hormones are released such as growth hormones and leptins which are important in metabolism and weight management. The brain, which never shuts off, is at least

Practical Application of the RESTORATION model:
Prescription for Health and Healing

able to rest during deep sleep since blood flow to the brain and metabolism slow down considerably. With proper sleep, one is subsequently invigorated and mentally refreshed.

Sleep deprivation can cause or exacerbate a variety of problems including mood problems, and stress which can complicate the battle against weight loss. As far as sleep, I recommend:

a. Get at least eight hours of sleep daily. The exact amount will vary between individuals.
b. Go to bed at least a couple hours before midnight. *An hour of sleep before midnight is worth several hours of sleep after midnight.*

c. Avoid going to bed on a full stomach, in a noisy environment or after consuming caffeinated products. All of these can interfere with the quality of sleep. Invest in a comfortable mattress.
d. It is easier to get a good night sleep after a busy and physically active day than one during which you were idle.
e. If you have difficulties falling asleep, contact your physician. Instead of settling for a sleeping pill, try to find out the underlying cause of your sleep disturbance.

2- Relaxation. Proper relaxation can be a powerful agent to combat stress. Stress is a common etiologic problem in obese individuals and should always be addressed. The mind cannot stay in overdrive all of the time. Without adequate relaxation, chronic stress, mood dysfunction and anxiety symptoms may develop, not to mention cognitive difficulties.

Somatic symptoms can also become evident if you consider that stress normally produces chemicals that affect organs of the body (brain, gut, lungs, heart and other muscles) adversely. Just like exercise can affect various functions in the body positively, chronic stress can also influence multiple bodily systems, albeit in a very negative way. When it comes to weight loss, stress must go!

3- Sabbath rest. Just as we require daily rest, the Bible teaches the necessity of having a weekly rest called the Sabbath. This is a type of rest that provides spiritual renewal and to which a blessing is attached (see Exodus 20: 8-11).

A – ACCOUNTABILITY

"Nothing in all creation is hidden from God's sight. Everything is uncovered and laid bare before the eyes of Him to whom we must give account."
Hebrews 4: 13

When it comes to obesity, you must first understand your condition. Genes play a role, sometimes a huge role in obesity. But so do many environmental factors that you can control. Do not hesitate to take

Practical Application of the RESTORATION model:
Prescription for Health and Healing

responsibility when you know you are at fault. Poor diet, a stressful lifestyle, lack of exercise, chronic anger and other negative emotions can all be the culprits. Acknowledging your shortcomings is the first step toward restoration. Only after the root of your problem has been identified, can appropriate steps be taken to prevent or correct it.

You do not need to be a medical doctor to understand the fundamentals of health and illness. The fact that obesity can lead to many problems is common knowledge. It is advisable to know everything that pertains to your own health and safety. It is in fact a solemn responsibility to understand the steps necessary to ensure your fitness. I recommend the following:

- ❖ Try to identify the cause of your obesity.
- ❖ Look closely at the following factors:
  - Your diet (quality, quantity and timing)
  - Stress level
  - Your relationships with other people
    - This includes family members, relatives and friends
    - Do you have a lot of enemies? Why? How are your emotions affected?
  - Spiritual life
    - Are you humble and forgiving?
    - Do you trust in God?
    - Is there is a sense of purpose in your life?
  - Self-image, self-worth, self-esteem
  - Activity level
    - Are you sedentary?

Practical Application of the RESTORATION model:
Prescription for Health and Healing

- ❖ Decide to take action *today*.
    - o Seek appropriate help
    - o Address any lifestyle and nutrition issues that may be present.

Never procrastinate when it comes to your health!

T – TRUST IN GOD

"Trust in the Lord with all your heart and lean not on your own understanding; in all your ways acknowledge Him, and He will make your paths straight."
Proverbs 3: 5, 6

Trusting in God is pivotal to the RESTORATION model. There are several reasons why, according to this model, it is important to trust in God:

- ❖ He created man. Therefore, He knows and understands the source

and solution to all our infirmities.
- ❖ God is omnipotent (all powerful). He can recreate, remodel, repair, and cure all our illnesses. He can speed up your metabolism, even if your genes dictate otherwise. You must do your part though and follow His health instructions.
- ❖ God has *your* best interests in mind, all the time. He is the only one that truly understands what your best interests are.
- ❖ By placing your full trust in God's ability to help you, you manifest faith, which is imperative when it comes to healing.
- ❖ You must have faith since "without faith, it is impossible to please God" Hebrews 11:6

Practical Application of the RESTORATION model: Prescription for Health and Healing

- The components of faith are:

  - **F-FEAR** the Lord, shun evil and live Uprightly.
  - **A**-Do not be afraid to **ASK**. Be bold in your request.
  - **I**-Be **INSISTENT**.
  - **T**-Have unwavering **TRUST** in God. Respect his **TIMETABLE**.
  - **H**-Only then can you expect **HEALING** and total RESTORATION

Trusting in God has an element of surrendering your will to God; that process is healthy and can provide peace. When healing occurs, it is important to give praise to God and to be thankful. If you really have faith, you can start the praise and thanksgiving before the healing is manifested.

I - INSIGHT

> "For I know my transgressions, and my sin is always before me."
> Psalm 51:3

Insight, hindsight and foresight should all go together. It is your responsibility to consider possible mistakes made in the past, assess the present, and take informed steps to ensure future wellness. Be your own medical detective. It is a fact that most obese individuals have problems that are related to lifestyle and nutrition. Many of these conditions are entirely preventable, and can be managed naturally. Understanding the source of your problem thoroughly and taking steps to correct it is

vital. It is important to *want* to lose weight and to be prepared to take the appropriate steps required. If you lack insight, you can always ask God and He will be only too happy to give it to you.

O – OPTIMISM

"So do not throw away your confidence; it will be richly rewarded."
Hebrews 10:35, 36

Optimism is always important. With optimism comes positive anticipation and hope. According to the RESTORATION model, you can be optimistic because the ultimate source of healing is God. He is certainly not lacking in healing power, wisdom, mercy, or understanding. Armed with this belief, you can step forward and engage in the activities that are necessary for weight loss to occur. If you are not optimistic, you will not put forth the effort necessary to get off to a good start. If you try and are not optimistic and should happen to fail the first or second time, you will easily give up. If you are not optimistic, each obstacle, real or imagined will appear colossal, each accomplishment will seem insignificant. By being optimistic, it allows you to set a goal ipso facto. Optimism is the path that can get you to your goal.

N – NUTRITION

> "Then God said, 'I give you every seed-bearing plant on the face of the whole earth and every tree that has fruit with seed in it. They will be yours for food.'" Genesis 1:29

Eating nutritiously is perhaps the natural law that is most often broken by individuals with an obesity problem. As far as weight

Practical Application of the RESTORATION model:
Prescription for Health and Healing

management, very little foods are neutral. There are foods that can promote weight gain, while others foods have the opposite effect. Beverages are the same. Some beverages, like water, can quench your thirst, cleanse and detoxify your body and not add calories. While other beverages, such as caffeinated sodas, can cause you to store unneeded calories, weaken your immune system, cause headaches and still not properly quench your thirst. The goal of nutrition should not only be to satisfy hunger, but to also meet the daily requirements of the body. When this is done, there should be no unhealthy cravings, weight gain, water retention or other types of disturbances commonly encountered. We should eat to live healthy and productive lives instead of living to eat.

I recommend the following:

- Drink approximately 8 glasses of water per day (more specifically, the amount of ounces equivalent to half of your body's weight in pounds).
- Eat plenty of raw fruits and vegetables daily. They contain live enzymes, fiber, antioxidants, minerals, vitamins, water and perhaps thousands of phytochemicals that are as yet unnamed, including other beneficial substances.
- Avoid dairy products. Substitute with soy/rice based products.
- Avoid caffeinated beverages and foods (chocolate) and red drinks.
- Avoid food additives such as MSG, nitrates, Aspartame/NutraSweet.

Practical Application of the RESTORATION model: Prescription for Health and Healing

❖ Avoid sweets. They are your number one enemy, even more than fat.
  o Consider eating low glycemic foods.
❖ Consider supplementation of your diet with antioxidants, essential fatty acids, glyconutrients, minerals, phytochemicals, and vitamins. Natural supplements are a much better and safer way to support weight loss compared to weight loss drugs that have the potential to cause severe adverse effects.

If you are confused and overwhelmed about which foods are best to eat and which ones may be contributing to your weight problem, just consider the following:

✓ You can never go wrong with foods that are fresh, raw, and are life-producing. The best

examples include fruits and vegetables that contain live enzymes to help you digest what you eat and other essential nutrients such as antioxidants, fiber, glyconutrients, minerals, phytochemicals, phytosterols, vitamins, and water. All of these help support weight loss while promoting health.
- ✓ You should be cautious of foods that are *decorated and treated* with unsafe chemicals and dyes but devoid of useful nutrients.

    o There is a difference between:
        - Corn on the cob versus corn chips
        - Fresh potatoes versus potato chips
        - Apples versus apple pie

- Carrots versus carrot cake

If you eats foods that are overly processed, this means that you are malnourished. You may be obese, and still be malnourished if you are eating the wrong kinds of food. Being malnourished can intensify or directly cause a variety of physical and mental health problems. It is impossible to lose weight effectively without addressing nutritional factors thoroughly.

Chapter 8: Conclusion

If you are obese and are thus not enjoying optimal health, there is still hope. God is the ultimate healer and will help you. He has provided simple health laws and natural tools that are innate and/or present in nature. These health *tools* are abundant, readily available, inexpensive, safe, effective and restorative. Following these health laws, which include proper nutrition, hydration, temperance, stress-free living, and spiritual renewal, you will experience total wellness.

While finding the right exercise program, buying the right healthy foods, and taking the right dietary supplements are all important for ultimate success to be reached, a total renewal is first necessary. You need to acquire strength and will power. You need to have a reason to be optimistic. In my case, as a health conscious physician, a brain specialist at that, I knew just what to do and was constantly plagued by the saying "*physician heal thyself*". There was a gap between my knowledge and actual application of that knowledge. It was not until I placed matters in God's hands using the principles of the RESTORATION model that I was able to get on the path toward success that resulted in my losing 100 lbs against all the odds after years of struggling.

More important than the weight I lost, was the realization that I was entirely transformed mentally and spiritually. In other words, I was totally restored. This can also be your experience by the grace of God.

Conclusion

"Praise the Lord, O my soul and forget not all his benefits. Who forgives all your sins and heals all your diseases, which redeems your life from the pit and crowns you with love and compassion, which satisfies your desires with good things so that your youth is renewed like the eagles." Psalms 103: 2-5.

About the author

Dr. Jean-Ronel Corbier is a Christian physician who is interested in wellness using an integrative approach. Although he is a specialist (he is board-certified in Pediatric Neurology), he felt the need to broaden his perspective regarding health and disease. Dr. Corbier's desire to be broad-minded medically started at Michigan State University where he enrolled concurrently in medical school and a graduate program in health and humanities. His studies in health and humanities provided him the opportunity to work with health practitioners who use a more holistic approach in treating patients. Dr. Corbier completed his neurological training at the University of Cincinnati and Children's Hospital of Cincinnati. He has done additional neurology training at Johns Hopkins and the Mayo Clinic. In particular, his Christian faith and strong spiritual background have enabled him to incorporate biblical principles in the treatment of his patients using a model that he and his wife, who is a pediatrician, have developed called the RESTORATION model. Dr. Corbier and his wife have one son, Jean-Michel, and they practice medicine in Montgomery, Alabama.

To order additional copies of:

Losing
100 pounds
Naturally

Call 334-418-0088
Or please visit our website
www.UfomaduConsulting.com

www.ingramcontent.com/pod-product-compliance
Lightning Source LLC
LaVergne TN
LVHW091933070526
838200LV00068B/953